You're God's Girl
Coloring Book

TEXT BY WYNTER PITTS
ARTWORK BY JULIA RYAN

HARVEST
Kids™

HARVEST HOUSE PUBLISHERS
EUGENE, OREGON

Scripture quotations are taken from...

the Easy-to-Read Version, copyright © 2006 by Bible League International.

the Holy Bible, New International Version®, NIV®. Copyright © 1973, 1978, 1984, 2011 by Biblica, Inc.® Used by permission. All rights reserved worldwide.

Cover by DesignByJulia

HARVEST KIDS is a registered trademark of The Hawkins Children's LLC. Harvest House Publishers, Inc., is the exclusive licensee of the federally registered trademark HARVEST KIDS.

YOU'RE GOD'S GIRL! COLORING BOOK

Text copyright © 2017 by Wynter Pitts
Artwork copyright © 2017 by Julia Ryan/DesignByJulia.com
Published by Harvest House Publishers
Eugene, Oregon 97408
www.harvesthousepublishers.com

ISBN 978-0-7369-6963-5 (pbk.)

Printed in the United States of America

23 24 25 26/ VP-JC /33 32 31 30 29

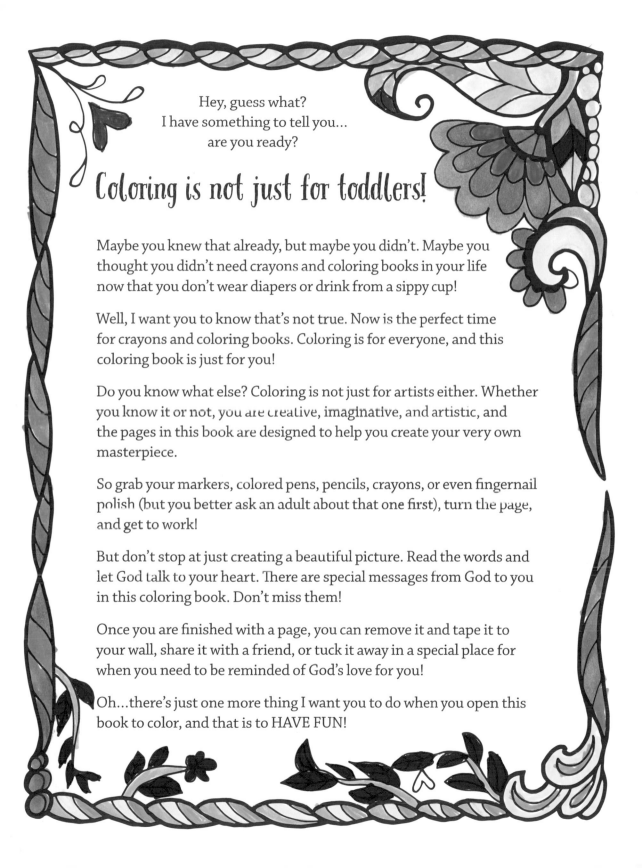

Hey, guess what?
I have something to tell you...
are you ready?

Coloring is not just for toddlers!

Maybe you knew that already, but maybe you didn't. Maybe you thought you didn't need crayons and coloring books in your life now that you don't wear diapers or drink from a sippy cup!

Well, I want you to know that's not true. Now is the perfect time for crayons and coloring books. Coloring is for everyone, and this coloring book is just for you!

Do you know what else? Coloring is not just for artists either. Whether you know it or not, you are creative, imaginative, and artistic, and the pages in this book are designed to help you create your very own masterpiece.

So grab your markers, colored pens, pencils, crayons, or even fingernail polish (but you better ask an adult about that one first), turn the page, and get to work!

But don't stop at just creating a beautiful picture. Read the words and let God talk to your heart. There are special messages from God to you in this coloring book. Don't miss them!

Once you are finished with a page, you can remove it and tape it to your wall, share it with a friend, or tuck it away in a special place for when you need to be reminded of God's love for you!

Oh...there's just one more thing I want you to do when you open this book to color, and that is to HAVE FUN!

Red 12/24/23

Finally, brothers and sisters, whatever is true, whatever is noble, whatever is right, whatever is pure, whatever is lovely, whatever is admirable — if anything is excellent or praiseworthy — think about such things.

Whatever

PHILIPPIANS 4:8

GOD'S LOVE is in ME

"If you remain in me and my words remain in you, ask whatever you wish, and it will be done for you."

JOHN 15:7

PSALM 19:14

May my words and thoughts please you. Lord, you are my Rock* the one who rescues me.

Dear God...

I SPEAK LOVE

EPHESIANS 4:29

I AM His

For we are God's HANDIWORK, created in Christ Jesus to do good works which GOD prepared in advance for us to do. EPHESIANS 2:10

GOD'S PLANS are GOOD now and later.

I HAVE GOOD PLANS FOR YOU. I DON'T PLAN TO HURT YOU. I PLAN TO GIVE YOU HOPE AND A GOOD FUTURE. JEREMIAH 29:11

You are the LIGHT that shines for the world to see.

MATTHEW 5:14

GOD sees me

"I saw you while you were still under the fig tree before Philip called you."

JOHN 1:48

JOY is in me!

I pray that the God who gives hope will fill you with much joy and peace as you trust in him. ROMANS 15:13

You are young, but don't let anyone treat you as if you are not important.

1 TIMOTHY 4:12

"LORD, IF IT'S YOU," PETER REPLIED, "TELL ME TO COME TO YOU ON THE WATER."

Crazy Faith

MATTHEW 14:28

God loves talking to me!

God says I am worth it!

MATTHEW 6:26

GOD Made Me Amazing

I am Fearfully and Wonderfully made. PSALM 139:14

My beauty is on the inside

Jehovah Jireh: God gives me everything I need.

Dear God, help me to stand out, not so people will see me but so they will see **You!**

I Know God is real because...

May the Lord bless you and keep you.

May the Lord smile down on you and show you his kindness.

May the Lord answer your prayers and give you peace.

NUMBERS 6:24-26

LET MY LIFE BE YOUR EXAMPLE

PROVERBS 23:26

"GOD"

God, you always know just what I need.

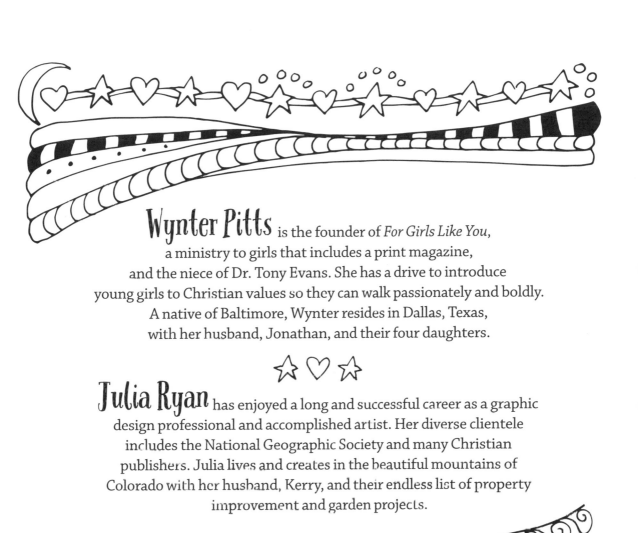

Wynter Pitts is the founder of *For Girls Like You*,
a ministry to girls that includes a print magazine,
and the niece of Dr. Tony Evans. She has a drive to introduce
young girls to Christian values so they can walk passionately and boldly.
A native of Baltimore, Wynter resides in Dallas, Texas,
with her husband, Jonathan, and their four daughters.

Julia Ryan has enjoyed a long and successful career as a graphic
design professional and accomplished artist. Her diverse clientele
includes the National Geographic Society and many Christian
publishers. Julia lives and creates in the beautiful mountains of
Colorado with her husband, Kerry, and their endless list of property
improvement and garden projects.

For information on more Harvest House coloring books,
please visit our website:

www.harvesthousepublishers.com